Fighting for Freedom

Written by Ian Morrison
Illustrated by Marjorie Scott

South Africa

Contents

Who Is Nelson Mandela?

Nelson Mandela is a great South African leader. He fought against laws in South Africa that were unfair to black people and other people of color. He wanted all South African people to be treated fairly. Mandela was put into prison for his ideas. After many years, he was released from prison. He later became president of South Africa.

1918

Nelson Mandela is born in a small village called Mvezo in South Africa.

1944

Mandela helps to form the African National Congress (ANC) Youth League.

1952

Mandela opens South Africa's first black law firm.

1962

Mandela is sent to prison for protesting against South Africa's laws.

Setting the Scene

South Africa

South Africa is often called the Rainbow Nation because of the many different colors of its people. For many years, white people ruled the country, even though most people in South Africa are black.

Nelson Mandela was born in 1918 in a tiny village like the one shown at right.

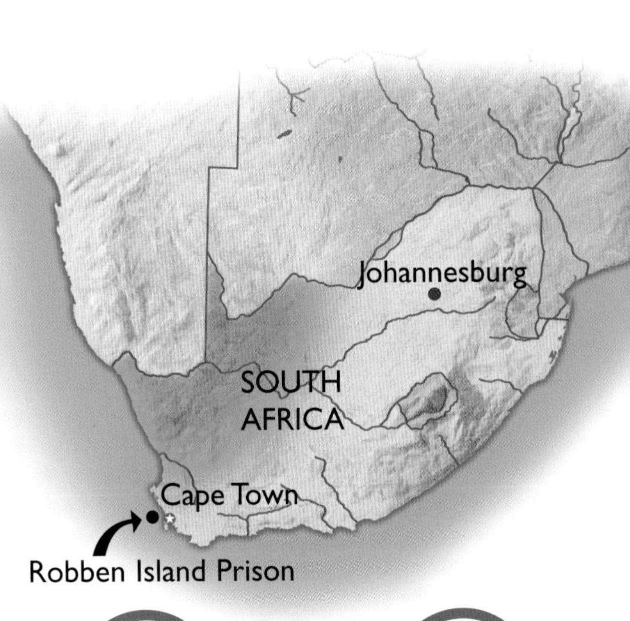

1990	1991	1993	1994
Mandela is released from prison.	Mandela becomes leader of the ANC.	Mandela receives the Nobel Peace Prize.	Mandela becomes the first black president of South Africa.

Early Days

1927

All morning, Nelson had herded cattle. In the afternoon he had gone to school. By nighttime, Nelson was tired, but he wouldn't miss Tatu Joyi's stories for anything. He loved to listen to the old chief's tales of African tribes in days gone by.

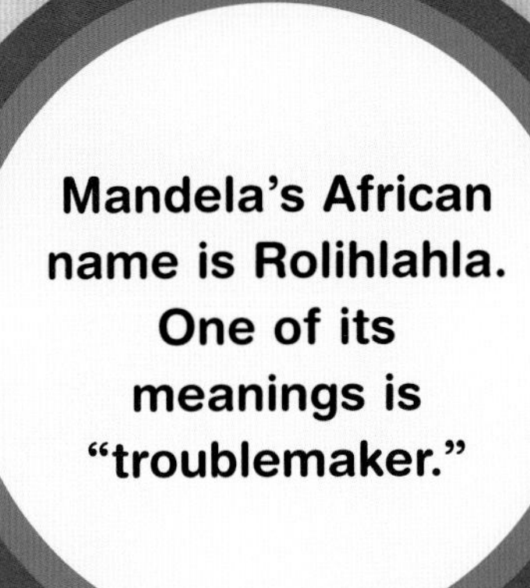

Village life in South Africa was hard. Boys like Mandela had to work most of the day, herding sheep and cattle in the fields. However, Mandela was lucky. Unlike many other children, he was able to go to school.

Nelson Mandela grew up in a part of South Africa called the Transkei (*trans KYE*). Today, many children in the Transkei still help take care of sheep and cattle.

Unfair Treatment

1941–1948

When Nelson was 23, he moved to Johannesburg to study law. He was shocked at the way black South Africans were treated there.

Nelson remembered Tatu Joyi's stories about white people's unfairness to blacks in earlier days. He remembered how bad the stories had made him feel. It seemed to him that nothing had changed since those days. Nelson made up his mind to change things himself.

In 1948, a system called apartheid (*uh PART hite*) was begun. Under apartheid, black people, Indian people, and other people of color were not allowed to vote. They couldn't live, work, or play sports with whites. Black people were forced to live in separate areas and give up their seats on buses to whites.

Mandela at age 20

Protest

1949–1960

Nelson passed his exams and became a lawyer. He opened an office to help black people who were in trouble with the law. Before long, people began to look up to him. He became a leader of the African National Congress (ANC), a group that fought against apartheid.

Nelson believed in peaceful protest. He urged people to disobey unfair laws, even if it meant they would be arrested.

protest to speak out or act against something you think is unfair

In 1956, Mandela and other members of the ANC were put on trial for treason. The trial lasted five years. In 1961, they were all found not guilty and were released.

During the trial, 156 people were accused of treason. Mandela is circled in red.

treason the crime of plotting against your country

On the Run

1961–1964

Nelson knew the police would soon come to arrest him again. He said goodbye to his family and went into hiding. He wore disguises so he wouldn't be found.

Nelson still worked hard for freedom and equality even though he was on the run. He secretly traveled to other countries to give speeches and talk to other leaders. However, when he returned to South Africa, he was quickly captured and put in prison.

equality everyone having the same rights and freedoms

In 1964, Mandela was sent to Robben Island Prison. It was said to be the worst prison in South Africa. Many other blacks who opposed apartheid were also sent there. Mandela became their leader.

This photograph of Mandela wearing traditional clothing was taken during his time on the run.

oppose to be against something

Prison Life

1964–1990

Life at Robben Island Prison was hard. All the prisoners were black South Africans, and all the guards were white. The prisoners had to live in tiny prison cells, and they were forced to break rocks all day. Nelson was allowed only one visitor and one letter every six months. He was not even allowed to go to the funerals of his mother and his son.

Even in prison, Mandela was not forgotten. People around the world began to protest against his imprisonment and apartheid. They joined together to try and convince the government to set Mandela free.

Mandela is shown above with his friend Walter Sisulu at Robben Island Prison. Sisulu was also a leader of the ANC.

imprisonment being in prison

Free at Last

1990–1994

Nelson never lost hope. After spending 27 years in prison, he was finally set free in 1990. He was now over 70 years of age. However, he never stopped trying to help his people.

In 1994, a general election was held. Black South Africans were allowed to vote for the first time. The nation voted for Nelson to become president of South Africa. Apartheid was finally over.

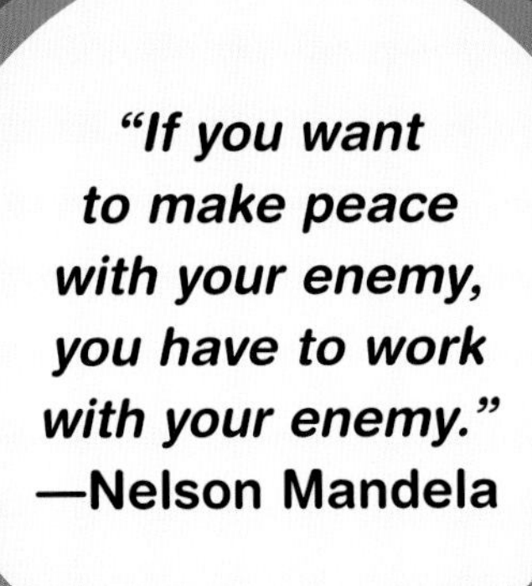

"If you want to make peace with your enemy, you have to work with your enemy."
—Nelson Mandela

The South African president F. W. de Klerk (1989–1994) had seen that apartheid wasn't working. He released Mandela and other ANC leaders from prison. Together, Mandela and de Klerk worked to bring an end to apartheid. For their hard work, they were given the Nobel Peace Prize, an award given each year to the person or people who made the greatest effort toward world peace.

Mandela and F. W. de Klerk receive their Nobel Peace Prizes in 1993.

Not Finished Yet

1994

Nelson had achieved so much. South Africa had become a democracy in which all people were equal and free. However, he was not yet finished fighting for the rights of others.

One night, Nelson met some homeless children in a street. He could see that they were cold and hungry. He decided to set up the Nelson Mandela Children's Fund.

democracy a country with a government that is chosen by all the people

"Children are the rock on which our future will be built."
—Nelson Mandela

Every year, Mandela gave one third of his pay to the Nelson Mandela Children's Fund. Many other people and companies also made donations. The fund gives money to groups that work to improve the health and education of children in South Africa.

Young people wave South Africa's new flag. The colors of the flag stand for the different cultures that now live in freedom in South Africa.

The Peace Parks

From 1999

Nelson stepped down as president of South Africa in 1999. However, he still works hard and supports many causes. One of these is the Peace Park Foundation.

Peace parks are areas in Africa where animals can safely roam between countries. They are called peace parks because countries have to work together to take care of the animals in the parks. In this way, people in those countries learn to understand and respect one another.

Not only do peace parks help save animals, but they can also help prevent wars. North Korea and South Korea have been fighting each other since 1950. Mandela has been working for the creation of a peace park that would join these two countries together.

The Siberian tiger is one of the rare animals that would live in a Korean peace park.

Mandela the Hero

Nelson Mandela is a true hero. He gave up his own freedom to help other people become free. Even after 27 years in prison, he was still sure that he could make a difference.

He began life as a village boy, and he became the president of South Africa. He is now over 85 years of age, yet he still puts the needs of others above his own.

Freedom for All

"There is no easy walk to freedom anywhere."
—Nelson Mandela

Many people have worked to help others gain their freedom. Nelson Mandela's personal hero was Mahatma Gandhi. Gandhi helped people in India gain freedom from British rule. Others who have fought for freedom are:

- Martin Luther King, Jr. (United States): worked to make laws fairer for African Americans
- Emmeline Pankhurst (England): fought for women's right to vote
- Lech Wałęsa (Poland): helped bring democracy to Poland

Mahatma Gandhi

What If?

During his time in prison, Nelson Mandela was the most famous prisoner in the world. People and governments everywhere called for him to be set free.

What if people in other countries had not banded together in protest? Would Nelson Mandela have been set free?

Index

courage being brave